"Rise & Be Healed!"

by
Benny Hinn

CELEBRATION
PUBLISHERS INC.

Scripture taken from the
Holy Bible, King James Version.

"Rise & Be Healed!"
ISBN 0-9629569-0-2
Copyright ©1991 by Benny Hinn

Published by Celebration Publishers, Inc.
P. O.Box 292
Orlando, Florida 32802-0292

Dedication

This book is dedicated to believers in need of a miracle from the hand of God Almighty. May the promises from God's Word contained within these pages bring life and truth to each reader, producing dynamic, unwaivering, bold faith to trust the "God of miracles" today!

Rise and Be Healed!

God desires that His children walk in health and be whole! He longs for His people to enjoy the riches of divine health and to know the joy of His healing touch!

Just as it was in Jesus' day when at the seashore of the Sea of Galilee signs and wonders and miraculous works were beheld, so it is today! The blind still receive their sight, deaf ears are still being opened, the lame still leap to their feet and walk. Signs and wonders still happen!

There is not now nor has there ever been a "day of miracles", a specific, limited time-frame in which God miraculously intervened in behalf of His children to do the impossible. No! Rather, I serve the "God of miracles", a gracious, loving, unchanging Divine Being who has and always will work the impossible in the lives of mortal man when we reach out to Him and ask in faith believing.

Over the past several years I have heard

many a well-meaning individual, while attempting to console someone suffering from pain or disease, make a statement regarding the "day of miracles", perhaps as a specific period of time on God's timeclock. Let me assure you that God does want you to be well, to enjoy health and life in its fullness. There is no such thing with God as a "day of miracles". Rather, He is the God of miracles! His promise to us for healing and health is the same to this generation as to any generation in the past.

God's ability or willingness to perform the miraculous is not confined to a certain timeframe in church history. He is unchanging and totally benevolent toward His children. His greatest desire is for His children to walk in health and to prosper, even as their souls prosper. However, many have no understanding — no truth — on which to stand to claim their miracle. They may "hope" for the impossible, but have no real understanding or strength from God's promises on which their faith can be grounded and established.

The Holy Spirit has put this project on my heart — to assemble the scriptures which deal with the topic of healing. Each of the scriptures contained in this book represents a promise from God's Word regarding your healing. I have put together this collection of scriptures so that you can know the truth about God's promises for healing, and the truth that you know *will* set you free!

Let me assure you that God does want you to be well, to enjoy health and life in its fullness. Fill your life and heart with God's promises and take Him at His Word. Trust Him today for your miracle by applying these scriptures to your life. Hide them in your heart and let them bring life to your soul.

As you read the following healing scriptures, let your faith abound and flourish; reach out and trust God for the miracle for which you are believing. Ponder these promises. Let the Word of God wash over your spirit to strengthen you, to encourage you to trust our wonderful "God of miracles".

God's Promises for Healing
Old Testament References

The first reference in the Bible which deals with healing is found in Genesis 20:17. This is the first scripture in which healing is mentioned. *"So Abraham prayed unto God: and God healed Abimelech, and his wife, and his maidservants; and they bare children."* This is the first physical healing recorded in scripture as a result of answered prayer.

Exodus 12:13 is the next record of God's promise for health. *"And the blood shall be to you for a token upon the houses where ye are: and when I see the blood, I will pass over you, and the plague shall not be upon you to destroy you, when I smite the land of Egypt."*

Ladies and gentlemen, as you read these scriptures which I have prepared for you, I pray that the Holy Spirit will quicken these words, that the Bible will become alive to you. May the Word be sent forth through these pages that you may be

9

healed.

In Exodus 15:26 the Bible promises: *"If thou wilt diligently hearken to the voice of the Lord thy God, and wilt do that which is right in his sight, and wilt give ear to his commandments, and keep all his statutes, I will put none of these diseases upon thee, which I have brought upon the Egyptians: for I am the Lord that healeth thee."* This promise for healing has two parts to it: the conditions and the promise. The conditions were extended to Israel and all those who chose to come under the covenant of God as it was given to Moses. The four-part command was to "diligently hearken to God's voice," to "do that which is right in His sight," to "give ear to His commandments," and to "keep all His statutes". If these conditions were met, God's promise to Israel was "I will put none of these diseases upon thee" and "I am the Lord that healeth thee". God is the healer of His people. In this portion of scripture God reveals Himself as Jehovah-Ropheka, Jehovah the healer or Jehovah, your physician. The reason that no sickness was found upon the children of Israel who met these conditions — those who were obedient to God's commandments — was that God promises here to be the healer of His people. He healed them all by His word to prove to them not only that He could heal them, but that He was willing to do so to fulfill his promises and covenants. He healed them all by His Word and there was not one feeble person found in all their tribes.

Sickness and disease were and still are a curse upon mankind due to their willfull disobedience to God's laws and commandments or to their lack of understanding of God's provisions regarding health and healing. Where there is no understanding regarding God's promises and provisions, there can be no faith to appropriate our inheritance regarding health and healing. Fill your heart and life today with God's Word. Know and understand His promises to you. Allow God to be Jehovah-Ropheka (Jehovah the healer) today.

This healing covenant actually continues in Exodus 23:25-26 where it says *"And ye shall serve the Lord your God, and He shall bless thy bread, and thy water; and I will take sickness away from the midst of thee. There shall nothing cast their young, nor be barren, in thy land: the number of thy days I will fulfill."* One additional condition is stated in verse 25 — "ye shall serve the Lord your God." The promise contained in this portion of scriptures is found in the last part of verse 25 — "I will take away sickness from the midst of thee." We are also promised a full life in verse 26 — "the number of thy days I will fulfill."

Exodus 23:25-26 states this wonderful

promise: *"And ye shall serve the Lord you God, and he shall bless thy bread, and thy water; and I will take sickness away from the midst of thee. There shall nothing cast their young, nor be barren, in thy land: the number of thy days I will fulfill."*

The story of Moses and the children of Israel in the wilderness is found in Numbers 21:8. When sickness struck the people of God, God then declared to Moses, *"And the Lord said unto Moses, Make thee a fiery serpent, and set it upon a pole: and it shall come to pass, that every one that is bitten, when he looketh upon it, shall live."* This serpent upon a pole is symbolic of Jesus Christ on the cross. The Bible says anyone who will look upon it shall be made whole. Ladies and gentlemen, if we look and see Jesus, we'll be made whole. The serpent on the pole was symbolic of Jesus becoming sin on the cross. Look to Jesus today and be made whole.

The Bible also declares in Deuteronomy 4:40: *"Thou shalt keep therefore his statutes, and his commandments, which I command thee this day, that it may go well with thee, and with thy children after thee, and that thou mayest prolong thy days upon the earth, which the Lord thy God giveth thee, for ever."* When we keep the Word of God and keep our eyes upon Jesus, healing will be ours continually.

Deuteronomy 7:15 states *"And the Lord will take away from thee all sickness, and will put none of the evil diseases of Egypt, which thou knowest, upon thee; but will lay them upon all them that hate thee."* Sickness does not belong to you. It has no part in the Body of Christ. Sickness does not belong to any of us. The Bible declares if the Word of God is in our life, there will be health, there will be healing — divine health and divine healing. There will be no sickness for the saint of God. If Moses could live such a healthy life, so can you. The Bible refers to Moses in Deuteronomy 34:7, *"And Moses was an hundred and twenty years old when he died: his eye was not dim, nor his natural force abated."* Just think about that for a moment — 120 years old, yet his eye was not dim or his natural force abated. You may ask, "How can that be?" Because the Bible says the Word of God brings life and health to you. The Word of God brings healing to your body. The Word of God strengthens you and keeps you strong. Moses was so healthy and at the age of 120 years he was so well that his natural force was not diminished. His natural force and strength were as great at the end of his life as in his youth. What a marvelous thing to know health and strength all your days.

The Bible goes on to declare some powerful promises. Joshua 14:10, 11 reflects a statement

13

made by Caleb. *"And now, behold, the Lord hath kept me alive, as he said, these forty and five years, even since the Lord spake this word unto Moses, while the children of Israel wandered in the wilderness: and now, lo, I am this day four-score and five years old. As yet I am as strong this day as I was in the day that Moses sent me: as my strength was then, even so is my strength now, for war, both to go out, and to come in."* Caleb said, "I am as strong now as when I was young." Why? Because he, too, had the Word of God in his life.

What a marvelous testimony. Caleb had enjoyed health all his life. People of God, divine health is better than divine healing! If you are trusting God today for a miracle, once that miracle is yours, trust God for divine health from that day on — expect to live a life overflowing with health and strength.

Look at this portion of scripture in Joshua 14:10 for just a moment. Remember that God always keeps His word and promises to men. It would have been totally impossible for Caleb to die in any of the preceeding 45 years — whether by war or sickness or any other cause — because God had promised that he would live to inherit the place where he had gone as a spy at the request of Moses. His statement regarding his strength were not just boastful words or a pretense on the part of an aging man. Rather, his

14

strength was long lasting because, following this point in his life, he stood against the giants that tried to take his inheritance and expelled them. Don't let the giants of disease and sickness rob you of your inheritance today. Cast them out of your life and claim God's promise of healing and health.

The Bible goes on to affirm a powerful promise in Judges 6:23. Perhaps you are desperate for a miracle. Your doctor may have told you that there is no hope and that he cannot do anything for you. Don't allow those words to grip your being. Reject them and trust God. I pray that this word will become life to you right now, even as you read these precious promises and that healing will be yours. *"And the Lord said unto him, Peace be unto thee; fear not: thou shalt not die."* Fear not, thou shalt not die. If the doctor has told you there is no hope, remember that there is hope with God. God says fear not, thou shalt not die. The plague that has struck your life will not remain but will leave.

In I Samuel 1:11-20 we find the story of Hannah and her prayer for a child. *"And she vowed a vow, and said, O Lord of hosts, if thou wilt indeed look on the affliction of thine handmaid, and remember me, and not forget thine handmaid, but wilt give unto thine handmaid a man child, then I will give him unto the Lord all the days of his life, and there shall no razor come upon his head. And it came to pass, as she continued praying before the Lord, that Eli marked her mouth. Now Hannah, she spake in her heart; only her lips moved, but her voice was not heard: therefore Eli thought she had been drunken. And Eli said unto her, How long wilt thou be drunken? put away thy wine from thee. And Hannah answered and said, No, my lord, I am a woman of a sorrowful spirit: I have drunk neither wine nor strong drink, but have poured out my soul before the Lord. Count not thine handmaid for a daughter of Belial: for out of the abundance of my complaint and grief have I spoken hitherto. Then Eli answered and said, Go in peace: and the God of Israel grant thee thy petition that thou hast asked of him. And she said, Let thine handmaid find grace in thy sight. So the woman went her way, and did eat, and her countenance was no more sad. And they rose up in the morning early, and worshipped before the Lord, and returned, and came to their house to Ramah: and Elkana knew Hannah his wife; and the Lord remembered her. Wherefore it came to pass, when the time was come about after Hannah had conceived, that she bare a son, and called his name Samuel, saying, Because I have asked him of the Lord."* Note that in verse 18 she was "no more sad". She was "no more sad" because she had the assurance in her heart that her prayer would be answered — that she would have the son for which her heart longed and for which she had prayed. She left with her heart filled with faith, trusting God for the answer. Verse 19 states "and the Lord remembered her." Imagine the joy and fulfillment that she experienced as she held Samuel in her arms — the manifestation of answered prayer.

The Bible declares in II Samuel 24:25 *"And David built there an altar unto the Lord, and offered burnt offerings and peace offerings. So the Lord was entreated for the land, and the plague was stayed from Israel."* Because of David's offering, the entire nation of Israel was spared from a plague. I believe that if we honor the blood, if we apply the blood and thank Him for our healing, the plague will not come anywhere near us.

In II Kings 4:33-35 we find, *"He went in therefore, and shut the door upon them twain, and prayed unto the Lord."* This is part of an account where Elisha brought a child back to life. Verse 34 continues *"And he went up, and lay upon the child, and put his mouth upon his mouth, and his eyes upon his eyes, and his hands upon his hands: and he stretched himself upon the child; and the flesh of the child waxed warm. Then he returned, and walked in the house to and fro; and went up, and stretched himself upon him:*

and the child sneezed seven times, and the child opened his eyes." What a tremendous miracle in the life of this child because of Elisha, a true prophet of God. He was diligent. He continued until the miracle came. God's miracle-working power is not limited to sickness. In this case it extended beyond death. Notice that Elisha lay his body on the child's body twice — once until the body became warm. After walking back and forth in the house, he returned to the room where the child lay. He lay upon the child once again until life was restored to the child's body.

The story of Naaman, the leper, is another remarkable account of God's healing power. *"Then went he down, and dipped himself seven times in Jordan, according to the saying of the man of God: and his flesh came again like unto the flesh of a little child, and he was clean."* (II Kings 5:14). In this miracle God also brought healing through Elisha. A child was resurrected and Naaman was cleansed from leprosy, both miracles because of the Word of the living God.

II Kings 20:1-11 shares the account of Hezekiah who was sick unto death. Isaiah the prophet came to him, prophesying his death, bringing a warning stating that he should set his house in order — in other words, get ready, man, you're about to die. *"In those days was Hezekiah sick unto death. And the prophet Isaiah the son*

18

of Amoz came to him, and said unto him, Thus saith the Lord, Set thine house in order; for thou shalt die, and not live. Then he turned his face to the wall, and prayed unto the Lord, saying, I beseech thee, O Lord, remember now how I have walked before thee in truth and with a perfect heart, and have done that which is good in thy sight. And Hezekiah wept sore. And it came to pass, afore Isaiah was gone out into the middle court, that the word of the Lord came to him, saying, Turn again, and tell Hezekiah the captain of my people, Thus saith the Lord, the God of David thy father, I have heard thy prayer, I have seen thy tears: behold, I will heal thee: on the third day thou shalt go up unto the house of the Lord. And I will add unto thy days fifteen years; and I will deliver thee and this city out of the hand of the king of Assyria; and I will defend this city for mine own sake, and for my servant David's sake. And Isaiah said, Take a lump of figs. And they took and laid it on the boil, and he recovered. And Hezekiah said unto Isaiah, What shall be the sign that the Lord will heal me, and that I shall go up into the house of the Lord the third day? And Isaiah said, This sign shalt thou have of the Lord, that the Lord will do the thing that he hath spoken: shall the shadow go forward ten degrees, or go back ten degrees? And Hezekiah answered, It is a light thing for the *shadow to go down ten degrees: nay, but let the shadow return backward ten degrees. And Isaiah the prophet cried unto the Lord: and he brought the shadow ten degrees backward, by which it had gone down in the dial of Ahaz.*" Here we find an incredible story of how prayer can change the course of events. Hezekiah was very ill and his death had been prophesied by Isaiah. As soon as he heard the prophecy, the Bible says that Hezekiah turned his face to the wall and prayed. He basically discussed the matter with God — perhaps even argued with God. He reminded God that he walked in truth and had served Him with a perfect heart. Hezekiah wept and cried out to God.

Before Isaiah even had time to leave Hezekiah's presence, God spoke to him again and said, "Turn around and tell Hezekiah that I have heard his prayer and I have seen his tears. Tell him: I will heal him. On the third day he will go up to the house of the Lord, I will add 15 years to his life, and I will deliver him and his city out of the hand of the king of Assyria. I will defend this city for My sake and for My servant David's sake."

If you need a miracle today, don't give up! Trust God for the answer. Regardless of the nature of your need, no matter what words have been spoken by your doctor, cry out to God and ask

Him to heal you. It *is* His will for you to be well and enjoy a life overflowing with health.

In II Chronicles 30 the Bible states that Hezekiah kept the Passover. And when he did, God's Word says *"and the Lord hearkened to Hezekiah, and healed the people."*(II Chronicles 30:20). When the Passover was kept, healing came to an entire nation. Ladies and gentlemen, when we keep the Passover, when we honor Jesus Christ, when we see His blood, there will also be healing in our lives.

Nehemiah 8:10 says, *"Then he said unto them, Go your way, eat the fat, and drink the sweet, and send portions unto them for whom nothing is prepared: for this day is holy unto our Lord: neither be ye sorry; for the joy of the Lord is your strength."* When healing comes to your body, when the power of God touches your life, that healing brings joy and strength to your life.

Job 5:18 declares: *"For he maketh sore, and bindeth up: he woundeth, and his hands make whole."* Verse 20 of that same chapter goes on to say: *"In famine he shall redeem thee from death: and in war from the power of the sword."* God states that His hands make you whole, and in famine He redeems you and sustains your life.

We find a powerful promise in Job 5:26. *"Thou shalt come to thy grave in a full age, like as a shock of corn cometh in in his season."* If Jesus

21

should tarry, God's Word says that you will not die with some sickness. Remember, God does not kill His children. He does not destroy His children. God is not willing that any of you should be sick. This promise (Job 5:26) indicates that if Jesus should tarry, you will come to your grave in a full age. The word *"full"* means a healthy age. This verse also uses the example of a shock of corn. Corn in its season is so ripe, so right, so healthy looking, experiencing the best and most purposeful existence. That should be a representation of you at a full or mature age.

Job 11:17 conveys a beautiful promise. *"And thine age shall be clearer than the noonday; thou shalt shine forth, thou shalt be as the morning."* The Bible declares here that when you are looked upon, when people observe you because of God's power and God's Word being evident in you, that your age shall be clearer than the noonday. Regardless of your age in earthly years, you will be as the noonday — the time when the sun is straight up, at its peak of brightness and beauty. The verse promises that you will be as the morning. What a marvelous thought — your age, your health will be bright like the sunshine and as healthy looking as the beautiful morning.

Job 22:21 states: *"Acquaint now thyself with him, and be at peace: thereby good shall come unto thee."* If you want good to come to your life, acquaint yourself with the Lord of hosts. Know Him and fellowship with Him.

Job 33:24-25 is one of my favorite scriptures in the book of Job on the topic of healing. *"Then he is gracious unto him, and saith, Deliver him from going down to the pit: I have found a ransom."* People of God, Jesus Christ was the ransom God gave to us. Because of that ransom "His flesh shall be fresher than a child's: he shall return to the days of his youth." (vs. 25). God is so gracious. God is saying to you that there is no need for you to go down into a pit of sickness and disease. Why? The ransom has been found. When you find Jesus, the Bible declares your flesh shall be fresher than a child's: you shall return to the days of your youth. Just think, return to the days of your youth — to enjoy all the blessings that are synonymous with youth! Health is promised to both you and me.

The Bible also calls sickness captivity. The scripture declares in Job 42:10 that the Lord delivered Job out of all his captivity. I pray that as you read these scriptures on healing with me that God will also deliver you from that sickness or captivity which has kept you bound. I pray that the anointing of the Holy Ghost will come through these printed pages to touch and deliver you from your captivity. *"And the Lord turned the captivity of Job, when he prayed for his friends:*

also the Lord gave Job twice as much as he had before."

David declared in Psalm 17:8,9: *"Keep me as the apple of the eye, hide me under the shadow of thy wings, From the wicked that oppress me, from my deadly enemies, who compass me about."* His prayer was that he would be kept from his deadly enemies. Are you aware that oppression is sickness too? David asked the Lord to keep him as the apple of His eye, to be hidden under the shadow of His wing from the oppression of his deadly enemies. Then he went on to say in verse 11 that these deadly enemies had compassed him about. Sickness wants to attack. The demon of sickness wants to attack, but God Almighty will keep you as the apple of His eye. Remember to keep His Word so that He will keep you.

The Bible goes on to declare in Psalm 23:1 *"The Lord is my shepherd; I shall not want."* If you make God your Shepherd, — if you follow the Good Shepherd, knowing the protection, provision, safety and blessings available to His sheep — you will never lack in your life. There will always be health.

Psalm 30:2 states *"O Lord my God, I cried unto thee, and thou hast healed me."* I pray that as you cry out to the Lord today, He will heal you, too. As you read the Word of God contained on these pages, I pray that He will bring healing to you.

Psalm 41:3 contains a wonderful promise for you: *"The Lord will strengthen him upon the bed of languishing: thou wilt make all his bed in his sickness."* The Lord will strengthen you upon your bed of languishing and God declares that He will make (in this instance the word "make" means turn) — and God will turn (or bring healing) upon your bed of sickness. Thank God for His mercy to us.

Psalm 91:10 promises *"There shall no evil befall thee, neither shall any plague come nigh thy dwelling."* How many times I have used that promise—over and over again. The Bible says no plague, no plague, no plague shall come nigh thy dwelling. No harm will ever come to you if you hide under the shadow of the wings of the Almighty.

Psalm 91:1 states *"He that dwelleth in the secret place of the most High shall abide under the shadow of the Almighty."* In that same Psalm in the very next verse we are instructed to declare that promise. For verse 2 says: *"I will say of the Lord, He is my refuge and my fortress: my God; in him will I trust."* In other words, when you hide under the shadow of the wings of the Almighty, you are to say to the Lord "You are my refuge, You are my rock, You are my fortress, in You, Lord, do

I trust. When you make this declaration, that is the time when God says, "No plague shall come nigh thy dwelling." So today declare the promises of God in your life, declare the Word of God so healing will come your way.

Psalm 103 begins with *"Bless the Lord, O my soul: and all that is within me, bless his holy name. Bless the Lord, O my soul, and forget not all his benefits:"* What are those benefits? *"Who forgiveth all thine iniquities; who healeth all thy diseases."* Saint, God declares He heals *all* your diseases. (The Bible sites a number of diseases and infirmities throughout both the Old and New Testaments which I have listed for your convenience and further study on page 53.) He promises to heal *all* — every one, any, any whatsoever, everything — all our diseases! That means not even a headache, sinus problem, not even a toothache — nothing! No sickness should come your way. God heals all your diseases. Then it goes on to say *"Who redeemeth thy life from destruction; who crowneth thee with lovingkindness and tender mercies; Who satisfieth thy mouth with good things; so that thy youth is renewed like the eagle's."* When health comes your way, the Bible says that your strength will be renewed like that of an eagle.

What a tremendous promise that is when you take a moment to examine some of the qualities and characteristics of the eagle. It is known to enjoy long life, some having lived over 100 years in captivity. Each year it casts off its old feathers and receives new ones, being renewed. Its strength surpasses that of any other bird. Because of its enormous wing span the eagle can soar so high, stretching its massive wings to catch the winds, lifting its body higher and higher. It can soar past mountain tops into the clouds and swoop very quickly back to earth. Its strength and endurance set it apart. Let your faith soar with the eagles today, being steadfast, unmovable, unwaivering and renewed.

Listen to what Psalm 105:37 declares about the children of Israel. *"He brought them forth also with silver and gold: and there was not one feeble person among their tribes."* He brought them forth and there was not one — not one — feeble among their tribes. When God took the children of Israel out of Egypt, the Bible says there was not one — not a human being, not a child, not a mother nor a father, no one was sick among all their tribes. There was not one sick among them because God healed them all at Marah (Exodus 15:26; Psalm 107:20). God's disposition toward His children remained unchanged. It is His will for us today to enjoy divine health. This is our promise under the new covenant, which is better in power and provision than the old covenant. Let's not be content to accept less than the children of Israel enjoyed. Expect to receive what has been promised to God's children—perfect health and perfect strength.

The Bible goes on now to declare in Psalm 107:20: *"He sent his word, and healed them, and delivered them from their destructions."* May this Word be quicked to each reader's heart today. He sent His Word and healed them and delivered them from their destructions. Even as I prepared this collection of God's promises for healing, I was sending His Word. The Bible says in Isaiah 55 *"My Word shall not return void."* As you read the words of these verses and they take root in your heart, faith is being birthed within you for the Bible says *"Faith cometh by hearing, and hearing by the Word of God."* (Romans 10:17). As you read these promises of God and hear them and hear them and hear them, your faith is released. Healing will come your way, for the Word is being sent your way. God will deliver you from all your destruction. Hallelujah forever more! What a wonderful God we serve!

Then the Bible declares another beautiful promise in Proverbs 4:20: *"My son, attend to my words; incline thine ear unto my sayings. Let them not depart from thine eyes; keep them in the midst of thine heart."* If the Word of God comes our way like this, then look with me at this promise — *"My son, attend to my words; my son, incline thine ear unto my sayings."* When the Bible says "attend," it says hear. But when it says "incline," it means don't be distracted when you hear. Don't let anything distract you from hearing what the Word says. Don't let anything else get in or take the place of what the Word is really saying. This portion of scripture continues in verse 21: *"Let them not depart from thine eyes; keep them in the midst of thine heart."* In other words, read it. Keep them in the midst of your heart. Protect it. "For they are life" — do you want life to come your way? Then hear the Word and don't let anything distract you from hearing it. Then the Bible says you must see it, you must read it. You have to protect it; don't allow it to be stolen out of your heart — *"for they are life unto those that find them and health to all their flesh."* (verse 22). It is my prayer right now that as your eyes gaze upon these promises from God's Word, as you read these scriptures and ponder them in your heart, that this word shall become life to you.

God's Word also promises healing for a broken heart. Often when we think about healing, we automatically relate it to a physical need. However, God's Word promises healing for non-physical needs — needs which may not be physically evident on the outside of an individual, but represent just as great an opportunity for a miraculous change in that life. Psalm 147:3 promises healing for the broken heart. *"He healeth the broken in heart, and bindeth up their wounds."* If you have ever had a broken heart and experienced a healing in that area, you know what a tremendous impact that renewal can have upon every part of your existence. God promises healing and restoration to the person who is suffering from a broken heart. Perhaps you are that individual. If so, reach out to our loving Heavenly Father today and claim this healing that is promised in Psalm 147:3.

Isaiah 33:24 states *"And the inhabitant shall not say, I am sick: the people that dwell therein shall be forgiven their iniquity."* They shall not say "I am sick". When the Word of God comes your way, you will not say, "I am sick." When the Word of God is heard, when the Word of God comes in, when the Word of God is read, when the Word of God is protected and health comes to all your flesh — I repeat, all your flesh — when this comes, then you can say what Isaiah declares in this verse — *"The inhabitant shall not say, I am sick."* Wouldn't you like that declaration to be yours? However, the Word of God must be in your life continuously. Don't lose the Word. Remember that hearing the Word brings life to you.

Isaiah 35:4-6 — *"Say to them that are of a*

fearful heart, Be strong, fear not: behold, your God will come with vengeance, even God with a recompence; he will come and save you. Then the eyes of the blind shall be opened, ears of the deaf shall be unstopped. Then shall the lame man leap as an hart, and the tongue of the dumb sing . . . " When you can say "I am not sick anymore" as Isaiah 33:24 declares, sickness will be gone. Don't let fear grip your heart. Trust God today and lean upon His promises. The eyes of the blind *shall* be opened — the ears of the deaf *will* hear — the lame man *shall* walk — the tongue of the dumb *will* sing!

Isaiah 40:28-31 says, *"Hast thou not known? hast thou not heard, that the everlasting God, the Lord, the Creator of the ends of the earth, fainteth not, neither is weary? there is no searching of his understanding."* (vs. 28) Man cannot weary the inexhaustible power of God Almighty. Our loving Father takes great joy in showering His abundant blessings upon His children. He is only wearied by the sin of rebellious man against His Word. (Isaiah 43:24: " . . . thou hast wearied me with thine iniquities.") *"He giveth power to the faint; and to them that have no might he increaseth strength. Even the youths shall faint and be weary, and the young men shall utterly fall: But they that wait upon the Lord shall renew their strength; they shall mount up with wings as*

31

eagles; they shall run, and not be weary; and they shall walk, and not faint." They shall mount up with wings as eagles. Eagles have an uncanny ability to "mount up", regardless of their age. The strength and endurance of the eagle is a dynamic example of the Christian's potential to overcome what could appear to be an insurmountable obstacle in the natural — perhaps some disease which medical science has labeled "incurable" or "terminal". Just as an eagle can soar up and over a mountain top to be enveloped by the sky, so can we "mount up" over our enemies of pain and sickness to be victorious. They shall run and not be weary, they shall walk and never faint. Oh my, what a marvelous thought! How precious these promises are!

Isaiah 53:4-5 — "*Surely he hath borne our griefs, and carried our sorrows: yet we did esteem him stricken, smitten of God, and afflicted. But he was wounded for our transgressions, he was bruised for our iniquities: the chastisement of our peace was upon him; and with his stripes we are healed.*" Do you know that the word "griefs" in the Hebrew which is *Kolae* means sickness, and the word "sorrows" which is *makob* means pain. So Isaiah 53:4 would read, "*Surely He hath borne our sickness and carried our pain.*" You shouldn't carry them today. Jesus of Nazareth carried them for you. Healing and health belong to you. Receive them.

Isaiah 58:8 — *"Then shall thy light break forth as the morning, and thine health shall spring forth speedily . . "* When Jesus Christ touches you, your light breaks forth as the morning and your health springs forth speedily. You will enjoy perfect health immediately.

Look at Jeremiah 8:22 now — *"Is there no balm in Gilead; is there no physician there? why then is not the health of the daughter of my people recovered?"* Balm — what does it symbolize in the Bible? The answer is healing. Gilead symbolizes worship. What this is actually saying is, "Is there no healing in worship?" God is asking a question. In other words, do you realize that when you worship, you will be healed? God is saying this. He says, "Don't you know there is healing in worship?" Why aren't you healed, why are you still sick? Perhaps because you have not worshipped. Worship brings healing, ladies and gentlemen. Why not stop for a moment and begin to worship Jesus right now for what He has done for you — for dying for you, for shedding His blood for you, for forgiving your sin and cleansing you from your unrighteousness. As you do, healing will come to your body.

Jeremiah 17:14 declares: *"Heal me, O Lord, and I shall be healed; save me, and I shall be saved: for thou art my praise."* When you praise

Him, when you worship Him, both healing and salvation will come. The prophet Jeremiah says, "Heal me, O Lord, and I shall be healed; save me, and I shall be saved." Why? Because you are my praise. I am praising you, I'm thanking you, I'm worshipping you, and as I am, I'll be healed. Ladies and gentlemen, I can sense an anointing even as I read over these scriptures while preparing them for you. This verse promises a two-fold blessing: physical healing and salvation.

Jeremiah 30:17 — *"I will restore health unto thee, and I will heal thee of thy wounds, saith the Lord."* When you worship Him, when you praise Him, when you exalt Him, when you thank Him for what He has done for you, the Bible promises that He will restore health to you, He will heal you of your wounds and your spirit will be renewed.

The Bible goes on to declare in Jeremiah 33:6: *"Behold, I will bring it health and cure, and I will cure them, and will reveal unto them the abundance of peace and truth"* God declares that when health and a cure come, peace and tranquility will follow along with contentment. Each of these are a blessing from God and cannot be artificially created or manufactured by man. They can only be given by God.

Hosea 11:3 states: *"I taught Ephraim also to go, taking them by their arms; but they knew not that I healed them."* Saints of God, Ephraim was taught and did not even know that he was healed. I am attempting to teach you through this collection of scriptures and pray that you will know deep within your heart that you are healed. The Bible declares that the work was done 2,000 years ago. God is not going to heal you now — he healed you 2,000 years ago. All you have to do now is receive your healing. Everything is complete; just receive it. Do you realize that the healing is here already? Jesus Christ healed you 2,000 years ago. All you must do today is receive it, take it, claim it. Praise Him for it right now!

The Bible declares in Nahum 1:13: *"For now will I break his yoke from off thee, and will burst thy bonds in sunder."* My, oh, my, when the Word of God is alive like this, when the anointing is so real, when the glory of God comes in, saint, that bondage of sickness shall be broken in your life. It is promised in the Word.

Just listen to this wonderful promise found in Malachi 4:2: *"But unto you that fear my name shall the Sun of righteousness arise with healing in his wings; and ye shall go forth, and grow up as calves of the stall."* Just think of that — when the Son of the Living God, called the Sun of Righteousness, arises with healing in His wings, the Bible says there will be growth and blessings in your life. "Ye shall go forth, and grow up as calves of the stall."

I pray that as we begin to review scriptures in the New Testament concerning healing, that same anointing of the Holy Ghost with which Jesus was anointed will touch your life, touch your body, touch your home.

Prayer of Faith

Holy Spirit, I thank You for Your Word. I thank you that the scriptures I have shared from the Old Covenant on each of the preceeding pages have brought life to each person who has read and pondered them in his heart. And now I pray that as we go on to examine your promises for healing contained in the New Testament, may the anointing of Your presence be experienced as it was experienced by so many of the great Bible heroes — Peter, Paul, John, James, the apostles and the disciples. Anoint each one, I pray. May this book bring healing and deliverance to each life in Jesus' name. Amen.

New Testament References

Matthew 8:1: *"When he was come down from the mountain, great multitudes followed him. And, behold, there came a leper and worshipped him, saying, Lord, if thou wilt, thou canst make me clean. And Jesus put forth his hand, and touched him, saying, I will; be thou clean. And immediately his leprosy was cleansed."* Ladies and gentlemen, saint of God, healing *is* the will of God for you. Never, ever, ever go to the Lord and say, "If it be thy will . . . " Don't allow such faith-destroying words to be spoken from your mouth. When you pray "if it be your will, Lord," faith will be destroyed. Doubt will billow up and flood your being. Be on guard against words like this which will rob you of your faith and drag you down in despair. It *is* His will. Jesus said, "I will". Let's believe Him and trust Him. Find out what the Bible says and then go to the Lord. Don't say, "If it be your will." Get to know what the Word of God promises, and you will see that it is God's will for you to be healed and enjoy health. Jesus told the leper, "I will" make you clean. Today He is saying to you, "I will". Be thou clean. Please notice something which is often missed. The Bible does not say that Jesus responded, "I will," and then put forth His hand. No, rather, he first stretched out His hand and then said, "I will". Do you realize that when Jesus did that, He was saying, "I want to heal you so much that I'll touch you, I'll deliver you, I will begin to heal you even before you will reach out to receive." Jesus was saying "I will," but I think there is something awesome and beautiful in the fact that Jesus touched him first and then said, "I will".

Mark 3:1-5 states: *And he entered again into the synagogue; and there was a man there which had a withered hand. And they watched him, whether he would heal him on the sabbath day; that they might accuse him. And he saith unto the man which had the withered hand, "Stand forth." And he saith unto them, "Is it lawful to do good on the sabbath days, or to do evil? to save life, or to kill?" But they held their peace. And when he had looked round about on them with anger, being grieved for the hardness of their hearts, he saith unto the man, "Stretch forth thine hand." And he stretched it out: and his hand was restored whole as the other."* In this we see that action is vitally important to a miracle. If you want God to grant the miraculous in your life for which you are believing—if you want Jesus Christ to heal you — you must act on your faith, you must release your faith, you must do something about it. This man stretched his hand and was made whole by the power of Almighty God.

Mark 5:25-34 tells the story of the woman with the issue of blood. *"And a certain woman, which had an issue of blood twelve years, And had suffered many things of many physicians, and had spent all that she had, and was nothing bettered, but rather grew worse, When she had heard of Jesus, came in the press behind, and touched his garment. For she said, If I may touch but his clothes, I shall be whole. And straightway the fountain of her blood was dried up; and she felt in her body that she was healed of that plague. And Jesus, immediately knowing that virtue had gone out of him, turned him about in the press, and said, "Who touched my clothes?" And his disciples said unto him, Thou seest the multitude thronging thee, and sayest thou, Who touched me? And he looked round about to see her that had done this thing. But the woman fearing and trembling, knowing what was done in her, came and fell down before him, and told him all the truth. And he said unto her, "Daughter, thy faith hath made thee whole; go in peace, and be whole of thy plague."* My, what a marvelous miracle; what a tremendous healing! This woman said, "If I can only but touch the hem of his garment, I will be healed." She came behind the crowd — such a vast crowd that it must have seemed as if a sea of people stood between her and her miracle. But she would not be denied. She persevered and as she pressed through the crowd and stretched out her hand, determined to touch the hem of His garment, she was made whole. This portion of scripture provides such a simple guide for each of us. In verse 27, she heard. Faith comes by hearing. Secondly, in that same verse, she touched the hem of His garment. She activated her faith. And then in verse 33 she came and told that she had been healed. These are three vital keys. First, she heard; second, she acted upon what she heard; and third, when she received her healing, she testified, "I have been healed!" When you hear the Word, faith is born. Faith cometh by hearing and hearing and hearing. When you activate your faith, the miracle comes. And when you tell someone, the miracle is kept. You keep what you have received by telling someone about it. That's why, when you are healed, don't ever keep it to yourself. Tell somebody that you have been healed.

Mark 10:46-50 declares *"And they came to Jericho: and as he went out of Jericho with his disciples and a great number of people, blind Bartimaeus, the son of Timaeus, sat by the high-*

way side begging. And when he heard (here again — he heard) *that it was Jesus of Nazareth, he began to cry out, and say, Jesus, thou Son of David, have mercy on me. And many charged him that he should hold his peace: but he cried the more a great deal, Thou Son of David, have mercy on me. And Jesus stood still, and commanded him to be called. And they call the blind man, saying unto him, Be of good comfort, rise; he calleth thee. And he, casting away his garment, rose, and came to Jesus.*" Please note just what was involved in blind Bartimaeus receiving his miracle. First of all, he cried out to Jesus for mercy. If he had not cried out to Jesus, Jesus would not have stopped to listen to the need of Bartimaeus. He would have just continued on His way. When you cry out to the Lord in faith believing for your miracle, He will stand still and all heaven will stand still on your behalf. Verse 48 says many charged him or threatened him to hold his peace — don't bother Jesus! Bartimaeus, be quiet! However, he would not stop. He would not give up; he was determined to make his need known. He cried all the louder. When Jesus heard him, he commanded that he be called to him. At this point Bartimaeus did an amazing thing—he took a step of faith and cast off his garment.

Now you may ask "just what significance does this have?" This was such a powerful act of

41

faith on the part of Bartimaeus. The garment which Bartimaeus cast off was the garment of the day which was worn by a blind person, granting him special considerations and privileges. Because of the garment, people would recognize that the person wearing it was blind and offer to help and assist him to his home, feed him, if necessary, and so on. Without that garment he could potentially starve to death. All blind individuals of that day wore that type of attire. When Jesus requested that they bring him, Bartimaeus threw away his garment and said by his action "I don't need this any more." That is truly faith. His act of faith in throwing away his garment before he received his sight was dynamic. He was confident that he would receive his sight. He knew that he knew that he knew he would receive his sight!

Perhaps you need to let go of the natural support systems on which you depend and allow God to miraculously intervene in your behalf. The unwaivering, determined faith of Bartimaeus was evidenced by his total lack of hesitation. Even though his garment was his insurance policy, his guarantee for his daily provision and everything he needed, he knew that what Jesus was able to give him was more desirable — more valuable — priceless. The Bible goes on to say in verse 51 *"And Jesus answered and said unto him,*

'What wilt thou that I should do unto thee?' The blind man said unto him, Lord, that I might receive my sight." Even though the Lord knew that he was blind, he still asked Bartimaeus what he desired. Bartimaeus had to make his request known by speaking it out. Many of us are not healed because we have failed to ask for our miracle. "Ye have not, because ye have asked not." Ask today — this moment — for your miracle. *"And Jesus said unto him, 'Go thy way; thy faith hath made thee whole.' And immediately he received his sight, and followed Jesus in the way."* He received immediately! An instantaneous miracle occurred in the life of Bartimaeus because of his total abandon to self and total faith in Jesus Christ.

Let's look at Luke 6:19 now. I pray that this will be a reality in your life today. *"And the whole multitude sought to touch him: for there went virtue out of him, and healed them all."* What a tremendous miracle — healed them all. It is my prayer today that you will be one of a multitude who, as they read these faith-inspiring words from God's Word, will receive your miracle.

Luke 17:11 states *"And it came to pass, as he went to Jerusalem, that he passed through the midst of Samaria and Galilee. And as he entered into a certain village, there met him ten men that were lepers, which stood afar off; And they lifted*

43

up their voices, and said, Jesus, Master, have mercy on us. And when he saw them, he said unto them, 'Go show yourselves unto the priests.' And it came to pass that as they went they were cleansed." As they went, they were cleansed! They were not cleansed from their leprosy until they went (until there was action); there had to be that act of faith. Today as you believe His Word and as you go (or take action), you will be healed and delivered.

Acts 3:1-8 — "Now Peter and John went up together into the temple at the hour of prayer, being the ninth hour. And a certain man lame from his mother's womb was carried, whom they laid daily at the gate of the temple which is called Beautiful, to ask alms of them that entered into the temple; Who, seeing Peter and John about to go into the temple, asked an alms. And Peter, fastening his eyes upon him with John, said, Look on us. And he gave heed unto them, expecting to receive something of them. Then Peter said, Silver and gold have I none; but such as I have give I thee: In the name of Jesus Christ of Nazareth rise up and walk. And he took him by the right hand, and lifted him up: and immediately his feet and ankle bones received strength." Notice, the man was not healed while he was seated. The man wasn't healed after he stood. Rather, he was healed *while* he was helped to stand. It took the act of faith again. Please notice what I am saying about the act of faith. With the lepers, as they went, they were healed. With Bartimaeus, healing came as he cast off his garment. The woman with the issue of blood was healed as she touched the hem of His garment. Here again, the crippled man seated at the gate called Beautiful was healed as he stood — action brought his miracle. *"And he leaping up stood, and walked, and entered with them into the temple, walking, and leaping, and praising God."* (vs. 8)

Acts 5:14 — *"And believers were the more added to the Lord, multitudes both of men and women."* When miracles began to happen, the Bible states that multitudes came because of the miracles. As miracles begin to happen in your life, you will begin to affect and influence people for God. They will come and say, "If you have received a miracle, maybe I will receive my miracle." God will use you as a mighty testimony. *"And believers were the more added to the Lord, multitudes both of men and woman. Insomuch they they brought forth the sick into the streets, and laid them on beds and couches, that at the least the shadow of Peter passing by might overshadow some of them. There came also a multitude out of the cities round about unto Jerusalem, bringing sick folks, and them which were vexed with unclean spirits: and they were healed every one."* Healed every one! Healed every one! That is my prayer today that every one will be healed today! I believe that the anointing is going to become so great that we will see signs and wonders such as those found in Acts 9:32.

"And it came to pass, as Peter passed throughout all quarters, he came down also to the saints which dwelt at Lydda. And there he found a certain man named Aeneas, which had kept his bed eight years, and was sick of the palsy. And Peter said unto him, Aeneas, Jesus Christ maketh thee whole: arise, and make thy bed. And he arose immediately. And all that dwelt at Lydda and Saron saw him, and turned to the Lord." I pray your miracle will turn many lives to the Lord starting today.

The Bible also declares in Acts 10:38 that God anointed Jesus of Nazareth with the Holy Ghost and with power. *"How God anointed Jesus of Nazareth with the Holy Ghost and with power: who went about doing good, and healing all that were oppressed of the devil; for God was with him."* Notice in Job 42:10 God called sickness captivity. And here it is called oppression. Ladies and gentlemen, if sickness is oppression, who wants it? I know you don't want it. That's why you are filling your heart and life with these

46

promises from God's Word. May the Word of God build faith in you to receive your healing today!

Then in Acts 14:9 — *"The same heard Paul speak: who steadfastly beholding him, and perceiving that he had faith to be healed. . ."* Here is a man from Lystra, impotent in his feet, being a cripple from his mother's womb, who had never walked. This man had never walked. Verse 8 states that. He heard Paul the Apostle speak. As he heard, faith was born. *"And Paul perceiving that he had faith to be healed, said with a loud voice, Stand upright on thy feet. And he leaped and walked."* What a tremendous miracle! The man, a cripple from birth, had never walked, but heard the Word of God and believed the Word of God. Paul saw it in the man's eyes and said, "Now get up and walk in Jesus' name," and the man did! Today I pray that the same power that flowed through Paul to touch that man at Lystra will also touch you to heal and deliver you from your problem.

Acts 19:11 goes on to declare much more to us. *"And God wrought special miracles by the hands of Paul: So that from his body were brought unto the sick handkerchiefs or aprons, and the diseases departed from them, and the evil spirits went out of them."* The anointing was so strong on his life that even handkerchiefs which had been rubbed on his body and distributed to the sick brought healing to the sick. It is that kind of anointing, saints, that breaks the yoke of bondage, even as Isaiah 10:27 declares.

Even as I compile these scriptures for you, I can sense the presence and anointing of the Holy Ghost so near. You are special to God and your body and its health are important to God. The Bible declares something very, very important that every Christian must realize and never forget. It says *"Know ye not that your body is the temple of the Holy Ghost which is in you, which ye have of God and ye are not your own; for ye are bought with a price; therefore glorify God in your body and in your spirit which are God's."* If your body belongs to God, it does not and cannot belong to sickness. This is found in I Corinthians 6:19. Your body is the temple of the Holy Ghost, and if it is the temple of the Holy Ghost, it's not the temple for sickness and disease. If your body belongs to God, it does not belong to sickness and disease. Today, as you read these powerful scriptures from the Word of God concerning healing, believe and receive what belongs to you.

Then in II Corinthians 4:10 it declares: *"Always bearing about in the body the dying of the Lord Jesus, that the life also of Jesus might be made manifest in our mortal body."* The Bible says that if we remember the cross, the Bible says that if we remember what He has done for us, it will be manifested in our body. This is why Jesus said "Take eat, this is my body broken for you." His body was broken that mine may be made whole. When we see the cross and we see what He has done for us, then the life of Jesus will be made manifest in our body. The Bible goes on to declare in verse 11 *"For we which live are always delivered unto death for Jesus' sake, — that is death to the flesh, death to the sins of this world — that the life also of Jesus might be made manifest in our mortal flesh."* Verse 10 says that the life of Jesus might be made manifest in our body. Verse 11 says that the life of Jesus might be made manifest in our mortal flesh. God wants His life and His healing power to be made manifest in your life and in your home.

And now the Bible says in Ephesians 5:23 that Jesus Christ is the savior of the body. He is not only the savior of the soul, He is the savior of the body. Ladies and gentlemen, you can cry out, *"You are the savior of my body, Lord Jesus, you are the savior of my soul."* If Jesus Christ is the savior of the body, then your body ought to be made whole.

James 5:13 declares *"Is any among you afflicted? let him pray. Is any merry? let him sing psalms."* If you are afflicted with sickness, the

Bible instructs you to pray — ask Him to heal you. *"Is any sick among you? let him call for the elders of the church; and let them pray over him, anointing him with oil in the name of the Lord: And the prayer of faith shall save the sick and the Lord shall raise him up; and if he hath committed sins, they shall be forgiven him. Confess your faults one to another, and pray one for another, that ye may be healed."*

The Bible goes on to declare in I Peter 2:24: *"Who his own self bare our sins in his own body on the tree,* (speaking of the cross) *that we, being dead to sins, should live unto righteousness: by whose strips ye were healed."* Ladies and gentlemen, your healing has already taken place. "By whose strips ye *were* healed."

The Bible declares in III John, verse 2, *"Beloved, I wish above all things that thou mayest prosper and be in health, even as thy soul prospereth."* In I Peter 2:24 it states "by whose stripes ye were healed." And we read here in III John that it is God's highest desire for you — God's greatest desire for the church of Jesus Christ — is that we be in total and perfect health. Why does health come? Listen to what the Bible declares in the following verses of III John — *"For I rejoiced greatly, when the brethren came and testified of the truth that is in thee, even as thou walkest in the truth. I have no greater joy*

50

than to hear that my children walk in truth." People of God, it is declared here why healing comes. It says *"Beloved, I wish above all things that thou mayest prosper and be in health, even as thy soul prospereth."* And then it goes on to say *"For I rejoiced greatly, when the brethren came and testified of the truth that is in thee, even as thou walkest in the truth. I have no greater joy than to hear that my children walk in truth."* Truth is mentioned three times in this passage of scripture. If you want healing and health in your life, get the truth in your life. God's greatest desire for you is that you walk in complete health. It will come when truth comes into your life.

Father, establish this word of truth today and confirm it in Jesus' mighty name.

Throughout this book I have given you the truth regarding healing and health. It is my prayer today that as you receive the word of truth it will bring healing to your life.

I agree with you today for your miracle and reach out by faith, trusting God for His healing anointing upon your life.

Prayer of Agreement

Father God, in the name of Jesus Christ of Nazareth, I agree with this reader for his/her healing and release the healing anointing upon each person who will read these promises from your Word. I command sickness to go, I command disease to go, bondage to go in Jesus' mighty name. Father, by the power of the Holy Ghost I pray that the anointing for healing will be released right now in Jesus' name and that from this moment on healing, restoration, and health will come to this dear saint. May the power and anointing of the Holy Spirit descend right now to bring total healing. This I pray in Jesus' wonderful and glorious name. Amen.

I come into agreement with Pastor Benny Hinn for my healing. I know that God is faithful to His Word and believe that His promises for healing will be manifest in my life. From this day on I will not doubt but will trust the "God of miracles" for my healing.

Signature _____

Date _____

"Who forgiveth all thine iniquities; who healeth all thy diseases;" (Psalm 103:3).

Diseases and infirmities named in the Old and New Testaments:

1. Barrenness *(childless)* — Genesis 16:1; Genesis 20:1-7)
2. Blindness (Genesis 27:1-2; Genesis 48:10; Leviticus 21:18; Deuteronomy 28:28)
3. Boils (Exodus 9:10; Deuteronomy 28:27)
4. Leprosy (Leviticus 14-15; Matthew 8:1-4)
5. Blemishes (Leviticus 21:18)
6. Lameness (Leviticus 21:18)
7. Flat nose (Leviticus 21:18)
8. Broken bones (Leviticus 21:19)
9. Crookedback (Leviticus 21:20)
10. Dwarfed (Leviticus 21:20)
11. Eczema (Leviticus 21:20; Deuteronomy 28:27)
12. Broken stones (Leviticus 21:20)
13. Scurvy (Leviticus 21:21; Deuteronomy 28:27)
14. Consumption *(wasting away, possibly cancer or tuberculosis)* — (Deuteronomy28:22-35; Leviticus 26:16)
15. Fever (Deuteronomy 28:22-27; Matthew 8:14)
16. Inflamation (Deuteronomy 28:22)
17. Itch *(general term for skin rash, sometimes viewed as a sign of leprosy)* — (Deuteronomy 28:27)
18. Burning ague (Deuteronomy 28:22; Leviticus 26:16)
19. Botch (Deuteronomy 28:17, 35)
20. Madness (Deuteronomy 28:28; I Samuel 21:15)
21. Sunstroke (II Kings 4:19-20)
22. Emerods *(boil-like swellings or tumours)* — (Deuteronomy 28:27; I Samuel 5:6)

Bible Diseases and Infirmities, Continued

23. Dysentery *(incurable disease of the bowels, perhaps chronic amoebic dysentery)* — (II Chronicles 21:12-19)
24. Atrophy *(wasting away of the body)* — (wasting away of the body) — Job 33:19-25; Psalm 102:5; Zecharaiah 14:12)
25. Sores and bruises (Psalm 38:5; Isaiah 1:6)
26. Venereal disease (Psalm 38)
27. Palsy (Matthew 4:24; Matthew 8:6; Matthew 9:1-6)
28. Demon possession (Matthew 4:24; Matthew 10:1-8)
29. Epilepsy (Matthew 4:24; Matthew 17:15)
30. Running issue (Matthew 9:20)
31. Dumbness *(voiceless, speechless, deaf or dumb)* — (Matthew 9:32)
32. Deafness (Matthew 11:5)
33. Dropsy *(not a disease in itself, but a sign of liver, heart, or kidney disease)* — (Luke 14:2)
34. Impediment of speech (Mark 7:32)
35. Ulcers (Luke 16:20)
36. Infirmity (John 5:5)
37. Worms (Acts 12:23)
38. Withered hand *(a hand in which the muscles are both paralysed and shrunken, leaving the limb thinner and shorter, deformed when compared to the other)* — (Matthew 12:10; Luke 6:6, 8)
39. Scab, spot *(a chronic disease which formed a thick crust on the head and would at times spread over the entire body)* — (Leviticus 21:20)

My Personal Study Notes

My Personal Study Notes

My Personal Study Notes

My Personal Study Notes

60

Audio teachings
by
Pastor Benny Hinn
on the topic of healing:

TAKING YOUR PLACE AND HEALING
THE SICK
(Catalog No. A112388)
$20.00*

A 4-tape series providing an inspirational overview of how to get your prayers answered and appropriate the healing power of God.

DIVINE HEALING, HEALTH AND LIFE
(Catalog No. A000702)
$35.00*

God said, "I am the God that heals you." This 7-tape series guides you in God's sytem of receiving healing and walking in divine health.

HEALING AND FAITH
(Catalog No. A000887)
$15.00*

This 3-tape series explains how to live in faith, receive and keep your healing.

BREAKING THE CURSE OF SICKNESS
(Catalog No. A052189)
$15.00*

Learn how to break the curse of sickness off you and and your loved ones with this 3-tape teaching series. Enjoy the blessing of God and live in divine health.

SETTING THE CAPTIVES FREE

(Catalog No. A072990)

$30.00*

Reverse the curse of sickness and poverty by learning to identify satan's "strongmen" to boldly triumph over demon powers.

For credit card orders call:
1-800-433-1900

or write to:
Benny Hinn Media Ministries
P. O. Box 90
Orlando, Florida 32802-0090

*(plus shipping and handling;
all orders are prepaid.)*